DEATHBED SEXT

CHRISTOPHER SALERNO

Winner of the Two Sylvias Press Chapbook Prize

Two Sylvias Press

Two Sylvias Press
PO Box 1524
Kingston, WA 98346
twosylviaspress@gmail.com

Cover Artist: Noela Kanecka
Cover Design: Kelli Russell Agodon
Book Design: Annette Spaulding-Convy
Contest Judge: Maggie Smith

Created with the belief that great writing is good for the world, Two Sylvias Press mixes modern technology, classic style, and literary intellect with an eco-friendly heart. We draw our inspiration from the poetic literary talent of Sylvia Plath and the editorial business sense of Sylvia Beach. We are an independent press dedicated to publishing the exceptional voices of writers.

For more information about Two Sylvias Press please visit:
www.twosylviaspress.com

First Edition. Created in the United States of America.

ISBN: 978-1-948767-11-8

Two Sylvias Press
www.twosylviaspress.com

Praise for *Deathbed Sext*

In the title poem, Christopher Salerno writes, "I want to waltz with you away from what// once was monstrously male/ about me and I also/ want to survive." The *and* here is crucial, and emblematic of the collection, which poem after poem says *yes, and*. Yes, high and low culture. Yes, both *sext* and *ghost* as nouns "you can verb." Yes, loving and leaving. Yes, familiar and strange; dead serious and absurd. "Everything is a piece of something else," Salerno writes, and everything gets to stay, because these deftly crafted poems are elastic enough to hold it all.

— **Maggie Smith,** Contest Judge and author of *Good Bones, The Well Speaks of Its Own Poison*, and *Lamp of the Body*

ॐ

The title nabbed me, the sext trope hooked me, but the poems—the poems—far exceed the nab and the hook. Numinous, masterfully crafted, rife with allusion, Salerno's lines mark the page with a surgical precision and delicacy. He pins back the flaps of masculinity, its privilege and its vulnerability, its lewdness and its fear, the unarticulated wound of it, "how some bruises/flower, spread like steam on the mirror/blurring all beauty." Without false heroics or glibness, Salerno enacts his own sexted desire: "May we become/to bravery what saying is to the sentence."

— **Diane Seuss,** author of *Four-Legged Girl* and *Still Life with Two Dead Peacocks and a Girl*

Acknowledgements

Many thanks to the following magazines in which some of these poems have appeared or are forthcoming:

American Poetry Review, "In Memoriam" and "Selfie With Sick Bacchus"

Bennington Review, "You'll Never Get To Sleep Now" and "Deathbed Sext"

Jubilat, "Post Op"

Los Angeles Review, "Horror Script"

New York Times Magazine, "In Vitro"

New Republic, "The Reenactment"

North American Review, "Horoscope for Gemini Men"

Plume, "Farm Stand During the Solar Eclipse" and "Moonshot"

Quarterly West, "Notes for Further Study"

Rhino, "Headfirst"

Willow Springs, "Men Who Won't Travel"

Table of Contents

"I used to have a cat, an old fighting tom, who would jump through the open window by my bed in the middle of the night and land on my chest. I'd half-awaken. He'd stick his skull under my nose and purr, stinking of urine and blood. Some nights he kneaded my bare chest with his front paws, powerfully, arching his back, as if sharpening his claws, or pummeling a mother for milk. And some mornings I'd wake in daylight to find my body covered with paw prints in blood; I looked as though I'd been painted with roses."

~Annie Dillard, *Pilgrim at Tinker Creek*

HEADFIRST

Just a boy then, I was struck
    hard by a car and arced over

the roadside. Despite the pain I told
    no one. How the man driving

kept on driving. I hadn't yet found out
    about the body or velocity.

What a wound is, and how some bruises
    flower, spread like steam on the mirror

blurring all beauty. My mother
    says the '80s were terribly rapey.

She hisses into her rotary phone.
    Says a man may leave his voice

inside of a stranger forever, place something
    hard as a blood-flecked stone.

When I woke in the road, I rested
    my little chrome bicycle by the curb.

The smell of lilac, the sound of traffic
    starting up again in the street.

Shapes that keep us awake decades
    later. The fuck do I know about

all this thickness? Not the slant rhyme
    of fear & underwear. Haven't I

walked around with a killer's power,
    swaggering until now? But any boy's

teen years: days spent pursuant to puberty.
    The body as factory. I would

have driven high across this enormous
        darkness just to watch a woman

unbutton air. I should be writing this
        with fear, knowing I was danger.

SELFIE WITH SICK BACCHUS

You climb a tree to eat the day's fruit
until the boughs crap out

> because your body must test the air
> to be art. Braid legs with branches

until the sun dulls. I am no docent
but so much depends upon

> proper diffusion of light. It's not
> the moon, though it pursues you. It's how

faces in paintings are lit like dead
relatives in dreams, their eyes

> pairs of dark gems. Caravaggio
> painted over several of his apostles

before giving Bacchus those sick eyes,
that crown of vines. We like this

> kind of art, but to buy it would cost us
> everything. Like listening to the story

of our own afterlife: once the stars
pull out and frost hits the field.

> Honey crystalizes in the jar.
> We vie for a view of something real—

oleander or our old selves—
but both contain poison.

DEATHBED SEXT

We always were the dying type.
Diagnosed early with *bon voyage*. As a boy
        I heard a murder
        ballad on the radio. Talk about
breaking the body into song!
        Like a budding sicko
I sang along. Beneath every boy's brainstem
        is a provisional gland. A full array
of rare emo registers
        Why a man in a barber's chair
        will stare deeply into his own eyes.
Comically big comb in the far corner of the room.
        It's just a life. One adjusts
        one's genitals in the empty elevator.
One adjusts
        a cluster of stars. When parts of us
need lifting up, I don't blame
        biology. But I wonder about
            our need for the irrational ritual.
        I watch M tape a clean
        maxi pad over the peep-
hole in her hotel door—
        is this about anonymity, not
        being seen? In our bodilessness
do *we* ever truly disappear?
        You can pay to receive

five texts a day that say, *Don't forget*

      you are going to die.

Device returned to its factory settings.

          The complete black of before.

What disquiets me now

      is not corporeal.

   It's the boredom on the faces

of the people on the streets

      of New York City.

   Send me pics of you eating a feeling.

   The three-layer cake of it.

I'm sending you the city at noon:

   day

      drunk

         brunch

     bros

  lower

     east

       side.

Young guy slips his elbow in jelly.

   Another puts a finger in his beer foam.

    Sidewalk dog startled

  by sudden saxophone. White

wrapper rising in

the puerile wind. Here's the condom I found

   on the floor of a midtown taxi.

One more dollop of lewdness

   for the fearhole. As kids we used

to talk about the fuck that flies,

  about the Hail Mary lay.

I want to waltz with you away from what

once was monstrously male

about me and I also

        want to survive.

You send me the forehead

with a palm on it.

      From the Met I send a photograph

         of an ancient Greek statue,

   the amazing arc of its ass

   lit by late-afternoon light.

Not even the gods look away.

AT THE FARMSTAND DURING THE SOLAR ECLIPSE

Aren't hens dear? How they squat
if willing to be picked up. Other-
wise, may run. *You know how it is*

says my most masculine friend.
To know a thing, we want to
touch it. I reach down to try a hen.

It scoots, wings raised like blades,
the sign for *no*. We've all seen them
sort of fly away: those mock-flights

that don't hold air. Embodying
perhaps our own flight patterns:
low over black water where the axe

sits lodged in the stump. I should be
less afraid of love. I hear
the laughter of women drifting

from the barn, see the changing sky
full-sized over the coop—a farm's
greatest truth. What I want to know:

how to fall out of love without
feeling like a fool. That's the dark
side of desire, I know, but we have

arrived here in time to witness
a rare solar eclipse. In the fields around,
acres of corn slap shut their husks.

Not even noon but the entire farm
is going dark, and every last hen,
from instinct, returning to the coop.

THE BYRONIC METHOD

There is no code or corrective shoe.
Only raspberries to cover the tips of my thumbs.

> When I sexted you a snorkel you sexted me a squid.
> Finally, a language for our modified love.

That spring I sexted the hell out of spires, ants on bananas,
some honeysuckle I saw in Syracuse. What else

> counterfeits like lust? A fire escape, a fluid sky.
> The endless ache of our minor works. I wanted to see

a distance, but through *your* eyes. When I sexted you
a telescope you sexted me the moon.

IN VITRO

More snow fell than was able
to be plowed. We turned
our faces to the clouds, waited
in waiting rooms to fill
out the forms, kissing each
one like the scalp of a child
with hair as unreal
as a doll built by hand
in the hold of a beautiful ship.
I sit in the room full of porn,
exhale my own name,
the one of that saint who
carried the Christ child
over a swollen river.

TEN WAYS TO KNOW HOW HE FEELS ABOUT YOU

When a man loves an omen
nothing can be done. You wait
all day to hear your name,
for the sentence and its syntax
to lie down together.

&

Your man puts a noun
where there is none. Animal
mineral vegetable sex. He takes
you to the river, makes a flat pebble
skip across the water.

&

Says he's living in an allegory, asks
that you wait for it to play out,
for the limits of his luck to take hold.
He hands you an afghan and a dented canteen
full of gin chilled to zero degrees.

&

While he's off buying stamps
you study the wallpaper:
faraway windmills rotating shyly
in a countryside. You rise,
try leaving, but the Victorian doorknob
comes away in your hand.

℘

Everything is a piece
of something else. The clothes
you remove like chaff, trying to hang up
your hang ups. A body is for
forming or for going,
he says, on a spree.

℘

Takes a girl by surprise. Using your wrist
as a hinge he spins you
on your heels, his leather cuff smudging
your smokey eye. You both
pitch south.

℘

But the era of omens isn't over.
All day he dreams of oxblood, runes,
Homeric doves flying
to the right. You say *only in music*
are there such heavy rests.
He hands you the hands of a clock
which you press into a book.

℘

Here is your lover in a larger pattern:
late-afternoon shadows on a sheet. The space
between clouds. The fluid
sky fat with joy
and also blue beyond reason.

&

He renames you *thee,*
asks *aren't we sparks?* At the dive
bar he sticks his finger
in your beer foam, dares you
to take him home.

&

The love leap, you think,
leaving your axis like you're in a ballet.
Perhaps tonight he will say your name.
But he comes riding a piano
into the room, begs you to listen
to his baritone vow.

MOONSHOT

I do have a past to break with.
Possibly in this very room full

        of heirloom geraniums that die
        unless we bring them inside, cut

each one back by half for winter.
We hope there is a future for

        delicate things. Poems of penance
        and limited logic written an hour

before the dark starts to exaggerate.
It's useful to say we have caused

        others to suffer. The moon glows whiter
        behind us in the mirror. And what's

the use of flying to the moon if we
are unable to cross the space that separates

        us from ourselves? May we become
        to bravery what saying is to the sentence.

This break in silence brought to you
by mistake in a room full of geranium

        pots hanging moonlike above. Where
        have we landed tonight? I take one

small, un-famous step toward my regrets
along the mind's white surface.

HORROR SCRIPT

At school we studied the mysteries
of the amygdala. The self

      and its contingencies. If you've ever
      cupped a lizard in your hands

you understand interiors.
Or a housefly, that little sinner no one loves—

      its greatest fear is not enough air.
      Many won't even make it till dusk

when whoever keeps calling
just breathes and hangs up

      and the dying fly on the windowsill
      buzzes to life again. All evening a black

Saab idles in your street.
Somewhere in the night you bleed

      on the sheets, wake again
      to your fear as a thing to rise into.

POST OP

A man I know receives ten bees
by mail each week.
His wife takes one by one
by the wings, lets them sting him
along the spine to raise
his body's total immune response.
How like a weed he must seem
to those bees, giving only a drop
of his sour blood back.
For months my mother had to turn
a tiny key to widen
the plastic palate glued
to the roof of my middle school mouth,
the year I told her I was ready
to raise myself. But when I woke
in the hospital after one more operation,
my stitches fiendishly itchy,
I wondered what history costs the body,
and if all our previous minutes
are still in us, why not roll
up the skin, squeeze
out all the air to make room
for more? Once the gauze
was taken off, layer upon oniony layer
removed, I was carried outside
where the ornamental cherry trees

of the upper east side
bloomed, and city bees seeking
certain immediacies burrowed
into the mouths of those flowers
trembling now from the weight
of all that frantic work,
and I begged each bee to sting
its strongly worded missive
into me in my post-op opioid haze.

IN VITRO

Then we froze the embryos like god
forsaken things. We wished upon

pharmaceutical stars. Never ask what fails
what it wants to be. Always *a vacancy*.

They filled our empty holes with needles
at autumn's end. They took our blood

which overflowed, formed a cold river
splitting two cities. It's hardly morbid

when nothing is even born. Later,
we'll go blind below the waist. Bodies

two nests swept from the eaves.
Yes, loss is full of new laws: I wake

each morning and in the space
between my legs a fruit bat hangs.

DICKINSONIAN PICS

I heard a phone buzz when I died.
Your sext lit up the larger darkness.
Bright as a swan or a wild syllable
lost to lust. How many men slip

into abandon, grow sick with kink. I had
taken my temperature, gotten one last look
at the zoomed-in moon, then felt
a vibration. I rushed to see the screen:

there interposed a photo of a lady
bug perched on the thong
of your sandal where it rested
from the stresses of the air. Maybe

there is too little structure
in seduction, like a loose scarf
taking to the sky. All day I look
out windows clouded by breath,
misjudge the nearness of lust & death.

YOU'LL NEVER GET BACK TO SLEEP NOW

At school we studied conquistadors. Ways masculine
    history could be measured in missions.
    My stepfather stepping
        through a cloud
           of boat motor smoke.
    Me gnawing this blue
pen into a shiv. Missions must be undertaken
        despite all futility:
I was sent to fetch a crescent wrench that wasn't even there.
    Soon, we learn to line up the tools.
    Locate gears behind tiny doors. Another poem
begins: we are building an enormous tugboat
      to crisscross the sound
     with only our unthinkable cargo.
   until we've become that
      someone on the farther bank who
       will never come back.
Having journeyed to the cape of no more feels, I kill
      a large Coke on the beach.
Today I walked backwards into the open sea
   pulling a wave over me like
       a wine-dark cape. On the sand
stood a bride and groom in a storm
   or divorce dream. At what age
   did I learn to swim all alone in the Atlantic
     even with my lack?
   Was I wanting to be so deeply startled
   I went in after dark?

To have an average heart

and be woken by thunder in the middle of

the night means

I'll never get back to sleep now,

so I go out where the morning is.

I'm trying to be more *woke* at work: acknowledgment of

weather coming in, souls afloat

in the chop offshore

of this wherever the hell.

With my steamer trunk

and my telescope, this is what I found:

When the world was flat as a finished proof

and men inched all night in wooden ships

floating just off the coast of newish worlds

there were mornings when the only things

to wake some men

in their dark harbors were the waves.

IN VITRO

Then the urologist says look
and I step into the beige corridor, peer
into the microscope where zillions
of my anonymized sperm freak, awake
from their thousand-year sleep.
I want to help the silly, frail
ones that veer like the bad shopping cart
with a shitty wheel, steering away
already from a world too full
as we head from winter into spring
to foghorns, pine sap, very
brave birds. Within an hour this batch
will be given a grade
for morphology, motility, then a rough
total count. Of those that would romp
until they wear themselves out,
only one will be injected into the egg,
the egg put back fat to try. One
more story about the stealth of *body.*
My eye against the microscope lens
is the beginning or the end.

ADVICE CONTAINING MOSTLY IMPRESSIVE BELCHES

Don't be the boy who eats things for money.
Don't listen at doors or you'll be seized
by the hair. Don't let the pitch of your voice
lift too high around other guys. As you reach
into your lover's coveralls beside the dead
poet's tomb, be sure to mention the monarch
butterflies, the tulips torn apart by fastidious
rain. If the conversation lags, don't say *a penis
for your thoughts.* It would be lovelier to say
the wine is on the table breathing. Personify desire
only when love threatens to do less. You must
carry a square of cloth to dab at the blood
should your zipper catch on the vestigial
genitals, place where your lover's words
once were. Didn't they ever teach you how
a word works? How its wings can operate
in any old wedge of sky as long as you be
a voyaging body. You can find your new
language in the *V* of a tree. Carve your new
initials into its thick trunk, male metaphor
of slow growing. To see a man without his hair
is nothing—to see a tree without its bark
is Sycamore. You must try not to speak
while your face is in lather. Stop sobbing
at parades. Never admit to mechanical
failure. When you say your final words of
the day to your new god, ask her to lay

her august thing down along the hate line.

Tonight, when the raccoons begin

to gather on the neighbor's roof at dusk,

light yourself some lamps. Before

it gets so dark you can't see your sewing.

HOROSCOPE FOR GEMINI MEN

Ghost is now a noun you can verb. Yet the best
a ghost can do is flick a light, whisper
I hate my afterlife. Maybe the problem is the fluidity
of identity, that *I* is too strong a word.
Gemini, as you walk away from another lover
you miniaturize, your body becoming a dot
of light on the horizon like the barely-visible
Venus. And what does all this leaving lead to?
Sigh. A body impossible to see. Hands
that miss you, the postcard of your neck
vanishing into the dark, the long bag you drag
through gravel stones. In another zip code
you open a beer, wonder what was desire—
the afterimage of form? And when the drapes fall
you sleep like a monk with your capacity
for suffering all the tears you provoke.
They say less wanting means more grace,
like running your finger along the fur
lining of an empty suitcase. Gemini, the heart
is wet, you are only sick. Brain swollen as
a nova above the rum and coke colored night
where even though these stars are dead
we still get to see them now and again.

MEN WHO WON'T TRAVEL

Snowplows
smack the manhole
all morning long.
Inconsolable crows
rise and reset. What
we have memorized
is moving again:
winter sun hitting
the substation fence—
a rubric for evening
as December strains after
its own vanishment.
Once the pigeons return
to the rooftops at dusk
having proven their part
in the natural history
of distance, I will eat
a pink grapefruit
from a faraway place,
pinch the little wooden
seed and whisper to it
the word, *Tallahassee,*
which is the name of
the city where they
discovered the sun.
I would like to go there

but I am impossible
to move, like a canoe
packed with snow,
a thing you only row
with your eyes.

THE REENACTMENT

What mattered in early wars
was the cavalry marching through
deep muck, the fife & drums,
stern ravens, words called out
across small, stagnant ponds.
They tell us every landscape longs
to be a battlefield. Someone
fires a cannon the size of a cave,
and we watch as shockwaves
italicize the trees. We, the living,
try channeling the original grief.
But this battle is nothing like
I thought it would be. I have little
idea what it takes to hold a field,
why someone might like to dress up
as the dead, those blown forward
in a crowd of men. Quick fuse:
young man with a bandage
and a period gun sings an anthem
from the archive, steps through
a cloud of cannon smoke.
White sight. A horse-drawn
darkroom rumbles by. A butterfly
flags. The gods never arrive.

THE DOUBLE IMAGE

I had sexted Anne Sexton and was stricken
with remorse & shamefacedness. No, this dream

> was not about the flesh-and-blood *Anne*
> Sexton, but about man's inner woman, the *Anima.*

They said I'd never get her back, not with my eyes
in keyholes or by waiting for something small

> to dilate. Everyone wants to know
> what I felt after she left me palimpsestic—

her outline still visible against the wall
like some painted-over apostle. But I only fell

> into endless confession like what the trees are doing
> right now budding out their forelocks

for spring. I stand to watch the forsythia in its flare,
and the season having its portrait done

> with such superlatives reminds me again
> how lost I am when Anne does not appear.

NOTES FOR FURTHER STUDY

You are a nobody
until another man leaves
a note under your wiper:
I like your hair, clothes, car—call me!
Late May, I brush pink
Crepe Myrtle blossoms
from the hood of my car.
Again spring factors
into our fever. Would this
affair leave any room for error?
What if I only want
him to hum me a lullaby?
To rest in the nets
of our own preferences.
I think of women
I've loved who, near the end,
made love to me solely
for the endorphins. Praise
be to those bodies lit
from gland to gland. I pulse
my wipers, sweep away pollen
from the windshield glass
to allow the radar
detector to detect. In the prim
light of spring I drive
home alone along the river's
tight curves where it bends

like handwritten words.

On the radio, a foreign love

song some men sing to rise.

IN MEMORIAM

An only boy may have

     had to play with god.

          Both of them beings

               as quiet as glue. I put

my nose to the sound

     hole in a mahogany guitar

          inhale the wood which

               never really dies. Like violets

pressed in a hymnal

     never die. Count me

          among those mourners

               singing all the wrong songs.

Christopher Salerno is the author of five books of poems and the editor of Saturnalia Books. His most recent collection is *Sun & Urn*, selected by the late Thomas Lux for the Georgia Poetry Prize at University of Georgia Press. His forthcoming book, *The Man Grave*, won the Lexi Rudnitsky Editor's Choice Award from Persea Books and will be published in 2021. Previous book include *ATM* (Georgetown Review Prize), *Minimum Heroic* (Mississippi Review Poetry Prize), and *Whirligig* (2006). His trade book, *How To Write Poetry: A Guided Journal*, was recently published by Callisto Media. His poems have been a recipient of the Prairie Schooner Glenna Luschei Award, The Founders Prize from *RHINO* magazine, the Two Sylvias Press Chapbook Prize, the Laurel Review Chapbook Prize, and a New Jersey State Council on the Arts fellowship. Other poems can be found in the *New York Times Magazine, New Republic, American Poetry Review, New England Review,* The Academy of American Poets series, and elsewhere. He lives in New Jersey where he is a Professor of English at William Paterson University in the BA and MFA writing programs. He can be reached at www. csalernopoet.com

Publications by Two Sylvias Press:

The Daily Poet: Day-By-Day Prompts For Your Writing Practice
by Kelli Russell Agodon and Martha Silano (Print and eBook)

The Daily Poet Companion Journal (Print)

Everything is Writable: 240 Poetry Prompts from Two Sylvias Press
by Kelli Russell Agodon and Annette Spaulding-Convy (Print)

Fire On Her Tongue: An Anthology of Contemporary Women's Poetry
edited by Kelli Russell Agodon and Annette Spaulding-Convy (Print and eBook)

The Poet Tarot and Guidebook: A Deck Of Creative Exploration (Print)

The Inspired Poet: Writing Exercises to Spark New Work
by Susan Landgraf (Print)

Deathbed Sext, Winner of the 2019 Two Sylvias Press Chapbook Prize
by Christopher Salerno (Print)

Crown of Wild, Winner of the 2018 Two Sylvias Press Wilder Prize
by Erica Bodwell (Print)

American Zero, Winner of the 2018 Two Sylvias Press Chapbook Prize
by Stella Wong (Print and eBook)

All Transparent Things Need Thundershirts, Winner of the 2017 Two Sylvias
Press Wilder Prize
by Dana Roeser (Print and eBook)

Where The Horse Takes Wing: The Uncollected Poems of Madeline DeFrees
edited by Anne McDuffie (Print and eBook)

In The House Of My Father, Winner of the 2017 Two Sylvias Press Chapbook
Prize by Hiwot Adilow (Print and eBook)

Box, Winner of the 2017 Two Sylvias Press Poetry Prize
by Sue D. Burton (Print and eBook)

Tsigan: The Gypsy Poem (New Edition)
by Cecilia Woloch (Print and eBook)

PR For Poets
by Jeannine Hall Gailey (Print and eBook)

Appalachians Run Amok, Winner of the 2016 Two Sylvias Press Wilder Prize
by Adrian Blevins (Print and eBook)

Pass It On!
by Gloria J. McEwen Burgess (Print)

Killing Marias
by Claudia Castro Luna (Print and eBook)

The Ego and the Empiricist, Finalist 2016 Two Sylvias Press Chapbook Prize
by Derek Mong (Print and eBook)

The Authenticity Experiment
by Kate Carroll de Gutes (Print and eBook)

Mytheria, Finalist 2015 Two Sylvias Press Wilder Prize
by Molly Tenenbaum (Print and eBook)

Arab in Newsland , Winner of the 2016 Two Sylvias Press Chapbook Prize
by Lena Khalaf Tuffaha (Print and eBook)

The Blue Black Wet of Wood, Winner of the 2015 Two Sylvias Press Wilder Prize
by Carmen R. Gillespie (Print and eBook)

Fire Girl: Essays on India, America, and the In-Between
by Sayantani Dasgupta (Print and eBook)

Blood Song
by Michael Schmeltzer (Print and eBook)

Naming The No-Name Woman,
Winner of the 2015 Two Sylvias Press Chapbook Prize
by Jasmine An (Print and eBook)

Community Chest
by Natalie Serber (Print)

Phantom Son: A Mother's Story of Surrender
by Sharon Estill Taylor (Print and eBook)

What The Truth Tastes Like
by Martha Silano (Print and eBook)

landscape/heartbreak
by Michelle Peñaloza (Print and eBook)

Earth, Winner of the 2014 Two Sylvias Press Chapbook Prize
by Cecilia Woloch (Print and eBook)

The Cardiologist's Daughter
by Natasha Kochicheril Moni (Print and eBook)

She Returns to the Floating World
by Jeannine Hall Gailey (Print and eBook)

Hourglass Museum
by Kelli Russell Agodon (eBook)

Cloud Pharmacy
by Susan Rich (eBook)

Dear Alzheimer's: A Caregiver's Diary & Poems
by Esther Altshul Helfgott (eBook)

Listening to Mozart: Poems of Alzheimer's
by Esther Altshul Helfgott (eBook)

Crab Creek Review 30th Anniversary Issue featuring Northwest Poets
edited by Kelli Russell Agodon and Annette Spaulding-Convy (eBook)

Please visit Two Sylvias Press (www.twosylviaspress.com) for information on purchasing our print books, eBooks, writing tools, and for submission guidelines for our annual book prizes.